UNSEEN

BRUCE LEE

THE REG SMITH CONNECTION

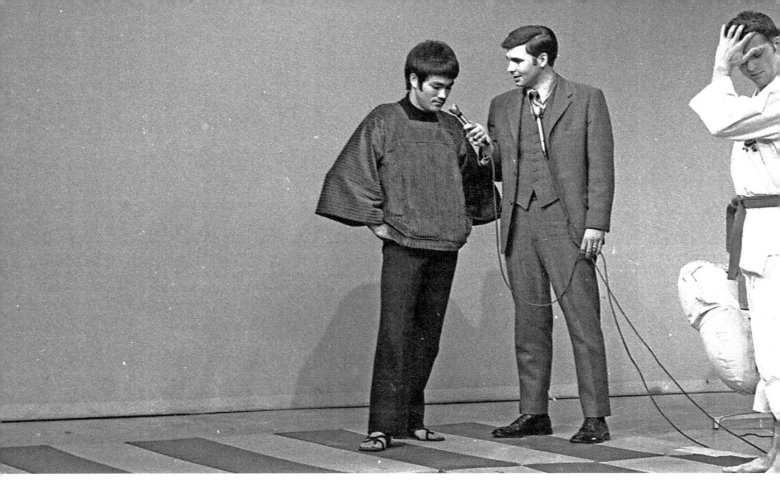

PRIMETIME TELEVISION

In October 1969, Bruce Lee embarked on a publicity tour for the MGM movie Marlowe in which he had a small co-starring role as hired thug 'Winslow Wong,' beside the popular Hollywood actor James Garner. The ten-day nationwide tour had stop-overs in Texas and Florida, the east coast to New York before finally heading westward-bound towards Los Angeles via San Francisco.

One particular stop on-route had Lee arrive at Charlotte Douglas International airport in North Carolina on Thursday, October 23rd. With a scheduled appearance on the local television channel, WSOC the following day, (as publicity for Lee's upcoming appearance in 'Marlowe'), MGM had recruited a local martial art expert to assist as part of a planned demonstration. The man in question was the renowned Taekwondo expert Reg Smith, who along with several of his students arrived that afternoon at the television studio.

Although footage from the afternoon television show has so far never resurfaced, a series of negative stills from the appearance, that hadn't seen the light of day since first taken, was recently rediscovered by Reg Smith, who thankfully had the foresight to capture during this now historical piece of Bruce Lee history. "If I recall, these photos were shot using TRI-X film," recalled Reg Smith. "This particular black and white film stock I used was ideal in a low-light environment."

In the accompanying pages, the reader will see this wonderfully captured moment in time, where Lee, unbeknown to not only himself, was on the eve of superstardom, and a few years later would become a household name worldwide.

So sit back and enjoy these wonderful images for the first time as 'Bruce Lee Forever' presents the Reg Smith photographic collection!

- Steve Kerridge 2020

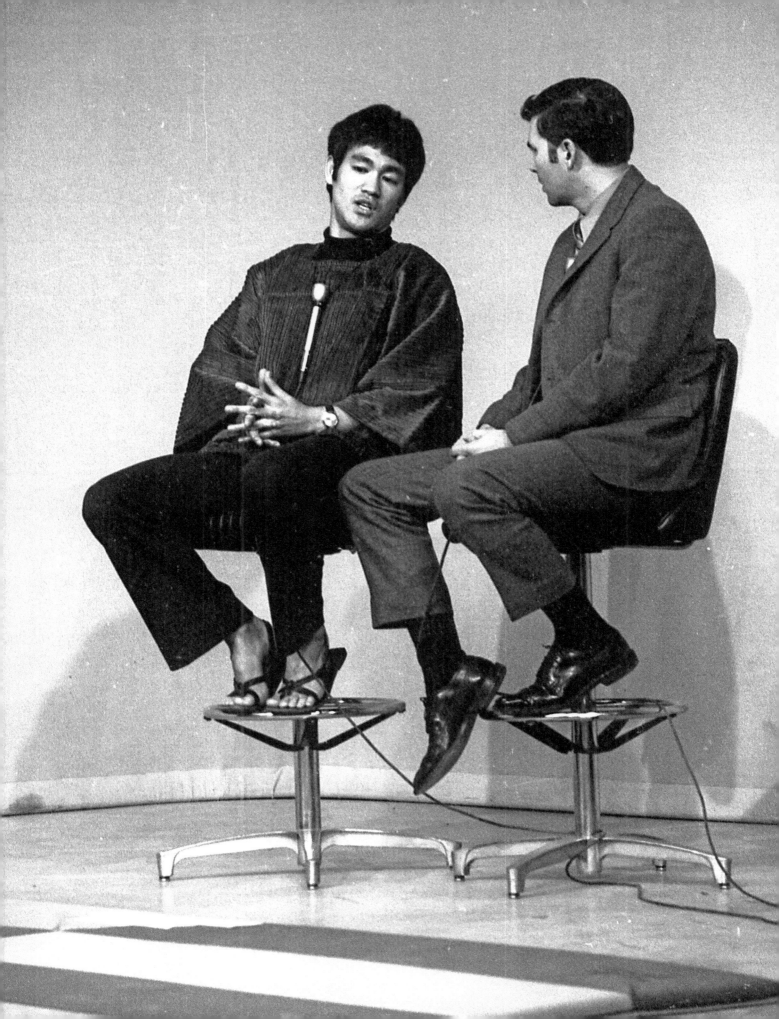

REG SMITH TAEKWONDO KWANJANG

IN HIS OWN WORDS

I'm often asked why I became so interested in martial arts. I grew up in the small town of Plymouth which is near the Outer Banks of North Carolina. I was a shy and timid child and was a target for bullies. And I was not very strong or confident. My initial interest was in learning self defense. Today I would like to thank those bullies for the wonderful path they put me on.

In high school I turned to weight lifting. Also ordered the few books available at the time on Judo and JiuJitsu. There were no instructors or schools back then. I practiced with a friend and we were amazed that "this stuff really works." A neighbor who had been stationed in Korea with the Army, told me about seeing men break bricks with their hands. I was fascinated ! My formal training began in 1961 when I entered the University of North Carolina at Chapel Hill. Most of my free time was spent training in Kodokan Judo and Shotokan Karate. Achieved brown belts in both.

In 1963, I started training in Taesoodo Jidokwan with Master Tae In Yun, an exchange student from Korea. Our school attended tournaments in the region from 1963 to 1965 and we prevailed at every one. I attribute this to the aggressive Korean kicking techniques we were taught. Most of the other styles were Okinawan or Japanese.

ACCOLADES

First North Carolinian to receive a Black Belt from Korea Taekwondo Assoc., Jan., 1965

Captain of first Karate/Taekwondo team at the University of North Carolina - Chapel Hill, 1963-1965

Opened the first Karate/Taekwondo school in Charlotte, North Carolina, U.S.A., 1968.
Promoted to 2nd Dan by GM Chung-Koo Kim.

Performed T.V. demonstration with Bruce Lee promoting upcoming movie 'Marlowe' in 1969.
Beginning of friendship with Bruce.

Was an official at the First Open International Karate Championships, New York, 1969.

Appointed as Educational Director of the (original) American Taekwondo Assoc., 1971

Promoted to 3rd Dan by the Kukkiwon through GM C.K. Kim, 1975.

Promoted to 4th Dan by GM C.K. Kim, 1979. Now running 2 schools.

Promoted to 5th Dan by GM Chong Woo Lee, through GM C.K. Kim, 1984.

Awarded Appreciation Citation from GM Chong Woo Lee for promoting Taekwondo Jidokwan, 1989.

Promoted to 6th Dan by GM C.W. Lee through GM C.K. Kim, 1993.

Took over a Taekwondo school in Hendersonville, N.C., after moving there in 1995. This was also the year
of the untimely death of my instructor for 30 years, GM C.K. Kim.

Promoted to 7th Dan by GM C.W. Lee through GM Myong Mayes of Fayetteville, N.C., 1999.

Appointed as President of Crime Stoppers of Henderson County, because of close association
with law enforcement agencies in 2001.

Selected by S.Korean government to go on a martial arts and cultural tour of Korea. Won a gold medal in Poomsae
at World Taekwondo and Cultural Expo, at age 65. Also spent a few days with GM Chong Woo Lee. 2008.

Inducted into Taekwondo Hall of Fame in New York in 2009. Was nominated by GM Al Cole.

Promoted to 8th Dan by Sung Wan Lee, President of Taekwondo Jidokwan, Korea, 2010

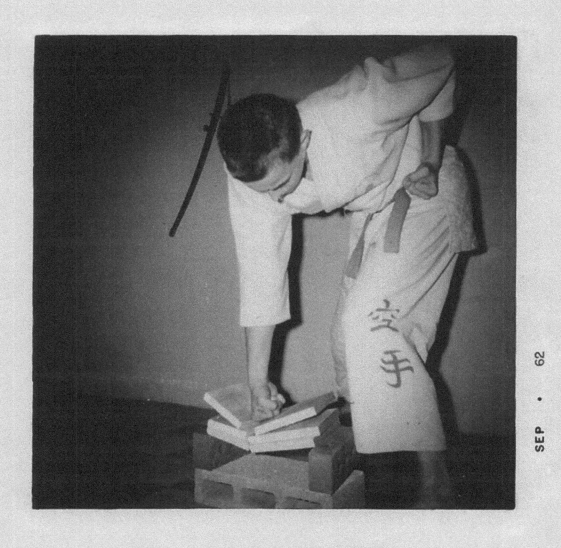

SEP · 62

Because of my prior training, I was captain of UNC's first competition team. Some of the tournaments we attended were at N.C.State, Duke University, Atlantic Christian College, East Carolina University, Camp Lejeune, Parris Island and Fort Bragg. Chapel Hill was not far from Fort Bragg and some soldiers from their club started training with us.

I consider this to be the Golden Age of Tournaments. There was no money involved. No fee to enter and no monetary rewards or trophies for winning. We got together simply because we loved what we were doing and wanted to compare styles. We all learned from each other. Later the promoters became involved and turned everything into big money-making events. Not that there have not been some good and very large tournaments, but it was never the same for me.

In 1964, Master Chung-Koo Kim came to America with help from my family. He became our head instructor at UNC. He was a former National Champion of Korea and was the most incredible fighter I have ever seen. When someone sparred him, they spent much of their time on the floor looking up at him. Master Kim had the most innovative takedowns I've ever seen before or since. He left me his original notes and diagrams, and if time permits I may produce a manual of his unique techniques.

In 1965, I was promoted to 1st Dan Black Belt. I was Master Kim's first black belt student and was the first North Carolinian to receive a black belt from the Korea Tae Kwon Do Association. The name "Tae Soo Do" was changed to "Tae Kwon Do" later in 1965. I'm told I have a rare early certificate. I moved to Charlotte, N.C., in 1966 to take a job as an insurance investigator. In 1968, I opened Charlotte's first Karate/Taekwondo school

at the Central YMCA. I also continued training with Master Kim, who was now in New York. In 1969, I was an official at Master Kim's "First Open International Karate Championships." This was a large event held at the N.Y. Hilton Hotel's Grand Ballroom. The guest of honor was Master Fumio Demura, a well known Japanese champion. Also in 1969, I had the pleasure of meeting Bruce Lee and we put on a T.V. demonstration to promote his new movie," Marlowe." Bruce and I became friends and I learned what a fascinating person he was. Not only for his innovative fighting style, but also the way he was greatly promoting martial arts for all of us. And he was kind, caring and had a good sense of humor. My Charlotte school kept growing and growing and I can thank Bruce for much of this. The Y was forced to give us an entire basketball gym for our classes. I had made an agreement with Bruce that the school would put on demonstrations at the theaters where his films were playing on opening nights. Our biggest event was for "Enter the Dragon" at the Park Terrace theater. This was a lot of fun and great publicity. Bruce and I continued to stay in touch, mostly by phone, until his untimely death in 1973.

I continued to teach Jidokwan style through the 1970's and opened a second school. And I was conducting some Saturday seminars at UNC-Chapel Hill. We introduced thousands of people to Taekwondo and produced several Black Belts. My first Black Belt student was Andy Jessup with the Mecklenburg County Police Department. Our classes have always been very traditional and we followed the same high quality standards of Korea. We also taught the philosophy, principles and strategy behind the martial arts, from Sun Tzu to Musashi. On the most basic level, it's about helping people to protect themselves. But after they've been doing this for awhile and develop some proficiency, the self defense motive starts to evaporate. A greater function is solving people's common problems such as overcoming fear and developing confidence for all aspects of life. Having the inner strength to overcome adversity because life is not always fair. It's given me the confidence and discipline to accomplish things in my life that I couldn't have done otherwise.

Top Left: Reg Smith breaking 3 one-inch boards with fist. Much Makiwara practice back then. This photo appeared on the front page of "The Daily Tar Heel," the UNC-Chapel Hill student newspaper, in 1962.
Above: The new school participated in Charlotte's annual "Festival in the Park," in 1968, putting on demonstrations every night. Instructor Smith is breaking boards with a flying sidekick.

Top: A rare photo of University of North Carolina's first Karate/Taekwondo team, 1964. Master Yun is front & center. Reg Smith was the senior student (red belt) & team captain (back row, 5th from right). In spite of an unprecedented record of dominating every tournament, the university gave them no recognition or support.

Bottom: This is the 1st Degree certificate Reg Smith received when he became the first North Carolinian to receive a Black Belt from the Korea Taekwondo Association, Jan., 1965.

Above: Reg Smith in 1968 after he had just been promoted to 2nd Dan by GM Chung-Koo Kim. He was about to open the first Karate/Taekwondo school in Charlotte, NC. Photo by Jane Styons Smith.

Below and Opposite (top): GM Reg Smith performing a six-foot-high jumping front kick (Twio Ap Chagi) circa 1960s.

Below: The Charlotte school grew rapidly because of the interest in martial arts, much of which was generated by Bruce Lee. The Y had to give us the main gym. Photo circa 1970-71.

Sometimes students feel apprehensive about promotion exams because of who they have to spar and compete against. Something I give them is this principle to meditate on: "Without fear, there is no courage." A deeper understanding of martial arts is that it's not just about defeating an opponent, but about overcoming one's own self. We are competing against ourselves. We are constantly striving to be better over time. And as we improve we are constantly winning. It's about being better than you use to be. You are a winner because you keep getting better. Stay on The Path. This is one of the reasons why martial arts is a way of life. The Way of the Warrior.

Traditional martial arts also has a moral culture. There has to be an ethical condition because we're playing with fire. It is about the correct conduct in life similar to the code of chivalry of the medieval knights. Our art should be like a "treasure in our pockets." No one sees it, but it is always there. And knowing that the best battle is the one not fought. In the 1980's we continued to expand and had a consolidated new location at the Harris Y in upscale South Charlotte. I also became a special instructor for the Mecklenburg County Police Department. My training continued with Master Kim and we attended several tournaments together. The " C.K. Kim Alliance" was formed and consisted of all of our association's schools, most of which were on the East coast. Master Kim conducted annual several day seminars which were usually held in Pennsylvania or North Carolina and they were video-taped. Charlotte had been growing at an out-of-control rate and became extremely chaotic for many reasons. It was time for my family and I to leave. In 1995, we moved to Hendersonville in the beautiful mountains of Western North Carolina. The Charlotte class was left in the very capable hands of senior student Malcolm Morris, who trained with us for a long time and exhibited an outstanding attitude.

This was the same year as Master Kim's untimely death, which came as quite a blow to all of us, but was also catastrophic for the Alliance of his schools. The infighting over power and control started in New York a year after his death. Many N.Y. black belts left our association and then the 2 people in N.Y.who were in control centered their attention on N.C. I'll not go into my fight with them as I've always hated martial arts politics. It goes against everything we are supposed to be living by. I had been asked to take over a Chung Do Kwan school in Hendersonville

Top: The first Karate/Taekwondo school was opened in Charlotte, North Carolina, U.S.A., by Instructor Smith in 1968.

Above: This was about a class on defending against multiple attackers. Instructor Smith is escaping from a bad position. Photo by "The Charlotte Observer," circa 1973.

Below: Reg Smith assisting GM Kim preparing lecture charts & notes at an Alliance seminar in 1993.
Opposite Top: In the 1980's we continued to expand & moved to a new location in upscale South Charlotte at the Harris Y.
This is our class about 1980. Many Black Belts.

Right:
Senior Grandmaster Chong Woo Lee and GM Reg Smith at the Kukkiwon in Seoul in 2008. GM Lee was GM Chung-Koo Kim's instructor.

because the instructor was retiring. This school was a part of the Henderson County Parks and Recreation Department. My time and energy went into this as I not only had the challenge of converting them over but upgrading their standards. I taught the traditional values of Jidokwan as well as the teachings of Master Kim, who had been my instructor for 30 years. I also introduced Bruce Lee's Trapping Hands and other parts of Jeet Kune Do. I had been studying Filipino Knife-Topping and Escrima/Kali which added a lot of fun to our classes. Assistant instructor Darlene Holbert was a major help with this school and she was promoted to 4th Dan. At this time I had limited interaction with only a few other branches.

In 2008, I was selected (along with 49 others in the U.S. and Canada), by the S.Korean government to go on a martial arts and cultural tour of Korea. It was the trip of a lifetime! Went to many historical sites, temples, monasteries and the DMZ. Not to mention the food! Entered Poomsae competition at the World Taekwondo and Cultural Expo in Muju and won a gold medal. I had just turned 65, and I was not in good shape at that time and was surprised that I won. The highlight of the trip for me was when we got to Seoul and I spent a few days with Grandmaster Chong Woo Lee, who had been Master Kim's instructor. I was

inducted into the Taekwondo Hall of Fame in New York in 2009. My son Ian accompanied me on the trip and was my photographer. I felt very honored and humbled that they selected me for this, even though they regarded me as a pioneer. Talk about being made to feel old! In 2015, I ended teaching classes and only give private lessons now. For my personal practice, my favorite training is with the Japanese Samurai sword. This practice is as much spiritual as physical for me.

We should all thank Steve Kerridge for his detective work in uncovering this aspect of Bruce Lee's history or this book would not have been possible.

- Reg Smith, 8th Dan

Top Opposite: This is the official document that must accompany the regular certificate for an 8th Dan promotion, which was received by GM Smith in 2010. This was from Sung Wan Lee, President, Taekwondo Jidokwan, Korea.
Opposite Middle: Grandmaster Chung-Koo Kim & Master Smith at a seminar in 1988. GM Kim was Smith's instructor for 30 years.
Opposite Bottom: On April 10, 2009, GM Smith was inducted into the TKD Hall of Fame as a "Pioneer" of martial arts in the United States. Photo by Ian Smith.
Below: GM Smith entered Poomsae competition at the World Taekwondo & Cultural Expo in Muju, Korea, and won a gold medal, at age 65.

In 1966, I was mesmerized by Bruce Lee who played Kung Fu expert Kato in "The Green Hornet" T.V. series. I was a new Black Belt and Kato was my hero, as the American public had not had much exposure to martial arts back then.

In my wildest dreams I never thought that I would ever meet "Kato," much less be in a T.V. demo with him and that we would become friends. Sometimes it still feels like a dream. When I think of Bruce today, the first image I have of him is as Kato.

- Reg Smith

INTER-OFFICE

MGM

TO **FIELD PRESS REPRESENTATIVES**

DATE **October 10, 1969**

SUBJECT **"MARLOWE"**

The following promotion tour has been set for Bruce Lee, karate star of "Marlowe:"

Monday	10/30	Los Angeles/Dallas	4:00PM	8:39PM	AA306
Tuesday	10/21	Dallas/Atlanta	7:05PM	9:49PM	DL38
Wednesday	10/22	Atlanta/Miami	6:06PM	7:35PM	DLA49
Thursday	10/23	Miami/Charlotte	3:00PM	4:36PM	EA736
Friday	10/24	Charlotte/Washington	8:35PM	9:35PM	EA388
Sat-Sun	10/25-26	Free Time - Washington			
Monday	10/27	Washington/Boston	6:00PM	7:18PM	NE330
Tuesday	10/28	Boston/Detroit	4:15PM	5:50PM	AA509
Wednesday	10/29	Detroit/Cincinnati	5:50PM	7:43PM	EL563
Thursday	10/30	Cincinnati/San Francisco	6:05PM	8:31PM	TW161
Friday	10/31	San Francisco/Los Angeles	6:15PM	7:16PM	UA539

I would suggest that since Bruce Lee can give an excellent demonstration of karate on television that you concentrate on this media, along with college, high school or other demonstrations. Radio interviews should be done in the hotel room. Be sure you contact your local karate/judo school for their cooperation. It is not necessary to use a limo or reserve a suite for Bruce Lee as he will be traveling alone. Special MGM Wants You To Meet Kits will be forwarded to you tomorrow. Please complete the local schedule and forward four copies to my office by October 15.

David McGrath

RECEIVED

OCT 14 1969

KARL E. FASICK

cc: Messrs. Terrell, Segal, Singer, Sheahan, Hatfield, Kallet, Golden, Walker, Cote

USA

SAN FRANCISCO

LOS ANGELES

DALLAS

DETROIT

CINCINNATI WASHINGTON

NEW YORK

BOSTON

CHARLOTTE

ATLANTA

MIAMI

DALLAS - ATLANTA - MIAMI - CHARLOTTE - WASHINGTON - BOSTON - DETROIT - CINCINNATI - SAN FRANCISCO

M.G.M. 'MARLOWE' PROMOTIONAL TOUR

OCTOBER 20th-31st 1969

"I might go on that publicity tour for MGM yet, though they are not too happy with the money I asked," wrote Bruce Lee to friend Jhoon Rhee. Planned for late October, the ten-day tour for M.G.M to publicise the upcoming release of Marlowe, would take Bruce Lee across the nation, covering Texas, Florida, the east coast and midwest, before reaching San Francisco, on his return to L.A. Throughout the tour, Lee appeared on several television and radio shows as well as giving several interviews for the many regional newspapers across the country.

"My participation was arranged by the MGM office in Charlotte, NC, to promote the Marlowe movie. I was selected because of my kicking ability (at the time). Bruce had a hard time against my kicks, but when he was able to move in with Wing Chun Trapping Hands, he tied me up

- Reg Smith

Karate Is Sissy Stuff ?

Kids, if you're wondering if the Green Hornet's main man Cato is really a top-notch karate expert, the answer is yes.

He's just a little guy, but he's fast like greased lightning and pretty smart upstairs, too.

Cato was in town recently as he was touring the Carolinas. His real name is Bruce Lee; he was born in Hong Kong 28 years ago.

One newsman wanted to know if he could break boards with a chop. "I don't chop, that's sissy stuff," said Bruce.

Not only doesn't he chop, but he doesn't use karate, either.

His brand of beat-em-up is called Jeet-kuno-do. One of the more specialized martial arts.

What's martial arts, one newsman wanted to know?

That's ways to beat up people, Cato told him in so many words.

He may not do too much chopping, but he's always glad to break up an office for you, like he does in a new movie he's in, without his Cato mask.

How about breaking somebody's necks, a newsman wanted to know?

"Ah, now you are talking," said Bruce, "that's something more concrete" (?)

This he can do. He also can blattey a 10-inch board with one good side kick.

Can a good dirty fighter beat up a good karate man? That depends on the man, says Bruce. "It's all in the attitude."

With the vast number of TV shows now in which women frequently bounce men off walls, the question of the day is can a woman really take a man who also knows how to fight.

The newsmen sighed with relief as Bruce assured them, "A woman can never ship a man."

Off the set, Bruce also runs martial arts studios and gives lessons himself — $500 for 10 lessons of 45 minutes each.

"What do you learn after that?"

"Oh, maybe how to give a good leg kick and then run like hell," Bruce launched over his peach compote.

Two of his students right now are Hollywood tough guys Steve McQueen and James Coburn. "McQueen's got potential," Bruce said, "He's got the real killer's instinct."

Bruce looks at his skill as an art that is the expression of the self. "It's like a waltz," he says. Waltz right up to somebody and reduce them to a box of bones.

Bruce works out every day to keep in shape. A newsman wanted to know if he imbibed?

"Nope, don't drink or smoke," said Bruce.

"No!"

"No. But I chew gum."

"Chew gum? How come?"

"Well, a lot of men smoke but Fu Manchu . . ."

Judo Expert Calls Hand Chop 'Stunt'

By EMERY WISTER
News Staff Writer

BRUCE LEE

Bruce Lee can break a six-inch board with one karate blow of his calloused hand, but shucks, he'd just as soon not.

"Just a stunt," snorts the expert on what he calls the Oriental martial arts. "How many times have you seen a board hitting you back? Now breaking a neck, that's more concrete."

Lee, who played the wiry Kato in the television series "The Green Hornet" a few years ago, was in Charlotte yesterday to promote the new motion picture "Marlowe." The movie, starring James Garner as Philip Chandler's famed private eye, casts Lee as a Chinese gangster who kills his victims by karate.

He comes to the Park Terrace Friday.

"Karate, judo, Aikido, I teach them all," says Lee who has his "chops" in Los Angeles, Oakland and Seattle. "I charge my students $500 for a 10 lesson course. But it takes a man at least 18 months to become proficient at it."

AND HOW does a person learn karate or any of the other defensive arts? Why, by being himself.

"The main thing is teaching a man to do his thing, just be himself. The individual is more important than style.

If a person is awkward he should not try to be able. I'm against trying to impose a style on a man. This is an art, an expression of a man's own self."

Anyway, after 10, 45-minute sessions the student has learned something, enough, he says, "to kick and run like hell."

"We have a lot more men than women studying the defensive arts now. In fact, I don't have any women at all at the moment. Women couldn't compete with men at this, anyway. I don't care what you've heard, there's no such thing as a 90-pound weakling tossing a 250 pound giant."

Lee gives a one-man demonstration of how to wreck an office in "Marlowe." Is a reasonably short, well-built man. He's a native of Hong Kong and has worked his karate magic on a number of television shows.

"I don't chop," he says describing his technique. "If I raise my hands to my shoulders I'll get several jabs from my opponent before I can get my arms down. For practice I would prefer trying to break a board hanging in a vertical position. I can break one from eight to 10 inches thick.

To see Lee's hands is to believe this. They are hard as pine. His knuckles are capped with calluses as hard as pine knots themselves.

"There's a secret in breaking a board with a karate chop," he said. "You have to go with the grain. If you condition yourself well enough and concentrate it will break."

Next spring or summer Lee will produce and play a featured role in a movie on the Oriental martial arts.

THE POPULAR star James Coburn, who had done a little karate fighting himself in pictures, will play the lead.

James Garner (left), dodges a karate kick by Bruce Lee in scene from "Marlowe."

Just Between Us

Murderous Feet Fly In New 'Marlowe' Film

By EMERY WISTER
News Entertainment Writer

Movies may be changing but the extra touch of gravy or gimmick is still the gravy for the sauciest flick.

There's a little gravy spilling over onto James Garner's new "Marlowe" picture. It is a diminutive Oriental named Bruce Lee who can kick the glass from a chandelier while standing on the floor.

WISTER

Lee is the karate king who added the spice to the "Green Hornet" TV series a few years ago. He is such an expert at the deadly game that he runs his own karate schools and goes all over the nation putting on demonstrations and showing his skill.

He's going on tour for "Marlowe" next month and MGM is mulling the idea of a Charlotte appearance. No doubt about it. His antics in the picture give the picture an extra punch, something it desperately needs.

"MARLOWE" is based on Raymond Chandler's novel "Little Sister" and Garner plays Chandler's dogged, hard-fisted private eye.

When he gets a little too close to the truth in a murder he is investigating, Lee turns up with a handful of cash to get him to lay off. When Marlowe refuses, Lee puts on a fantastic karate exhibition aimed at silencing the detective once and for all.

In the course of his shenanigans, Lee virtually demolishes Marlowe's office. There's absolutely nothing new about the bit nor the way it is brought off.

The police arrive just after Lee leaves; proving, I suppose, that movies are just movies and that things are done just the way they've always been done.

WALT DISNEY has been doing the same thing for years. Remember that movie in which Dean Jones and Suzanne Pleshette played man and wife with a houseful of young dogs? In one scene the pooches went on a playful rampage and literally destroyed the room, barking and yelping like mad.

Only after they had completed their comic destruction were they interrupted by their outraged owners, even though the couple was in the house with them and could have arrived at the scene almost at the first yelp.

This is a case where realism was rejected as impossible or at least not desirable. I differ a little with the movie-makers there.

The scene went on too long and, funny as it must have been to many people, it was inconceivable that someone did not put the shush on the dogs. Likewise, I wondered why the police did not take after the murderously destructive Lee in "Marlowe." Thus, after all, is no comedy.

Anyway, Lee puts on a fantastic display of karate prowess. It's more than exciting; it's downright frightening.

ROBERT MITCHUM has been telling friends he's retiring from movies after his current "Ryan's Daughter," but nobody's listening. Just let an actor of any merit at all say he's quitting and he's bombarded with a raft of good scripts. I think actors say this just to get better offers and it often works . . . The Rev. Billy Graham will pop up on Woody Allen's TV special tomorrow even though, as Allen says, "We agree on nothing." By the way, Allen's new movie "Take the Money and Run" is a corker. One big laugh from beginning to end.

. . . That "Under the Yum Yum Tree" TV series was dead almost from the minute it was made. The ABC stations liked it but the network brass said no . . . Much of the filming was done in a house on Malibu Beach and the man next door spent much of his spare time on the set. Name: Brian Keith . . . Would you believe James Mason is a Western? Columnist Hand Grant says he'll cross the Atlantic to do it, making his first Hollywood appearance in 12 years.

Throughout the ten-day promotional tour, the press ran coverage on the many appearances made by Lee across the country. To most, at this moment in time, Lee was still the television character 'Kato,' manservant to the Green Hornet, a 'top-notch 'Karate' expert as reported in the 'Gastonian Gazette' on November 5th, the week following Lee's appearance in the region on WSOC Television.

Several articles from the Charlotte newspapers held the same misinformed view by referring to Lee's martial art practice as 'Karate,' or, as one report from the 'Charlotte News' described, 'A Judo Expert.' Thankfully, Lee was given a platform in the article to express a brief synopsis of his approach to martial art when interviewed by reporter Emery Wister. "The individual is more important than style," explained Lee. "I'm against trying to impose a style on a man. This is an art, an expression of a man's own self."

WSOC-TV
CHARLOTTE CHANNEL 9

Friday October 24th 1969

My association with **Bruce Lee** began in October of 1969.

The MGM office in Charlotte, North Carolina arranged for me to be in a television demonstration with Bruce on WSOC, Channel 9.

This was to promote the new movie "**Marlowe**" starring James Garner and Bruce.

I was selected because of my kicking ability and high flying kick reputation, an attribute taught to me by my Taekwondo instructor, Master Chung Koo Kim. I was very excited about this opportunity as I'd long admired Bruce as "Kato" in the "Green Hornet" TV series. I had no idea I'd ever meet him or be in a demo with him.

Before the demo, Bruce and I spent a little time together privately at the Central YMCA where my school was located. This was just down the street from where he was staying.

Bruce wanted to go over what I planned to do in the demo as he was curious about my kicks.

He had been studying Taekwondo kicking with Master Jhoon Rhee. One thing led to another and we ended up doing a little informal sparring. At first, I controlled the situation by keeping him at kicking distance. That didn't last long. Bruce moved in on me and tied my arms up with techniques I'd never seen before. He wouldn't show me how he did it. I was very curious about this and the footwork he used to come in past my kicks and close the gap.

Left and Opposite:
Bruce Lee in trendy kaftan top, flared slacks and sandals in conversation with WSOC sportscaster and anchorman, Bob Lamey.

Below and Opposite:
Bruce Lee with WSOC sportscaster
and anchorman, Bob Lamey introduces Lee's
planned martial art demo with
one of Reg Smith's students.

Jhoon Rhee taught Bruce Lee his trademark step (skip) behind sidekick that he often used to kick the air shield. Bruce later taught it to tournament champion Joe Lewis who put it to good use. This had been a favorite Taekwondo sparring technique in my arsenal as well.

Above: Lee demonstrates the explosive power of his side kick as one of Reg Smith's students feels the full force while holding an air shield as show host Bob Lamey watches in amazement.

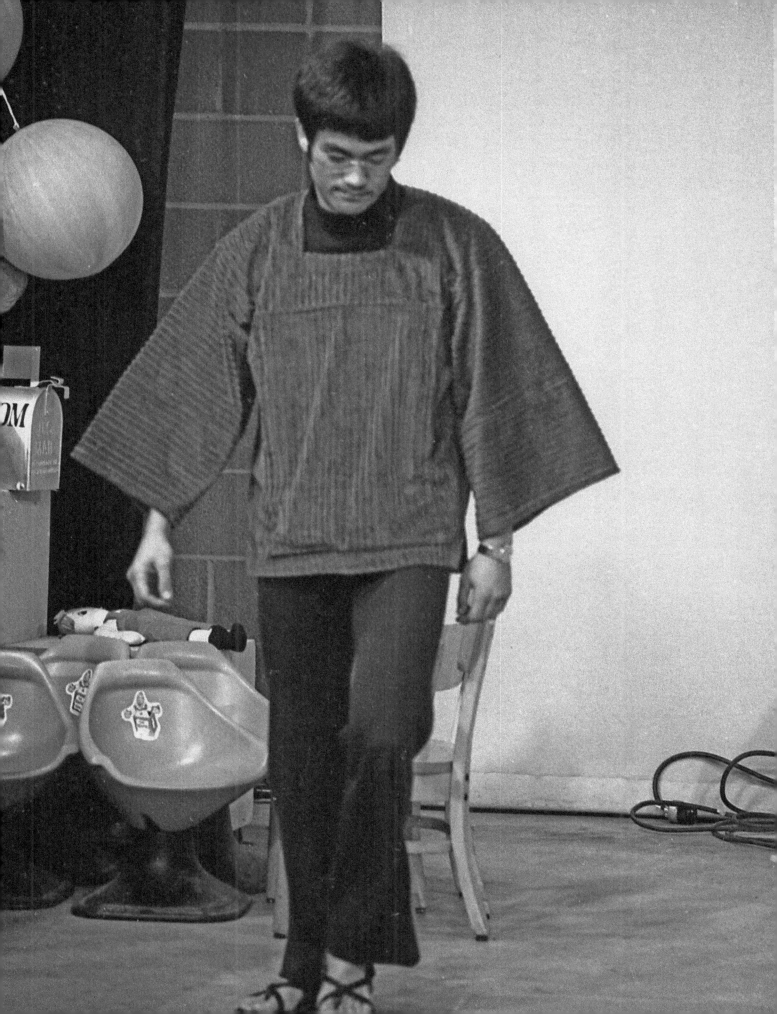

Left: Bruce Lee and studio staff observing the proceedings, as Reg Smith (facing camera), and one of his students position the safety mats prior to filming the demonstration.

"

In phone conversations with Bruce, he told me that the three main components of Jeet Kune Do, were Wing Chun Gung Fu, Taekwondo kicking and Filipino boxing. And the greatly misunderstood concept of 'broken rhythm' that he was teaching he got from an early book on European Fencing. I was able to find this book through a book-search company.

Bruce had been learning Taekwondo kicking techniques from Jhoon Rhee. I had worked out a few times at Rhee's school when visiting the Washington, D.C, area.

"One of my senior students,
Howard Herman was there to help.
He assisted Bruce in warming up for
the demo by holding the air shield.
Howard was on the receiving end of
several powerful kicks.

I demonstrated basic karate attack and defense techniques with another student as Bruce narrated.

Bruce and I had gone over the sequences in an earlier meeting. The demo went well.

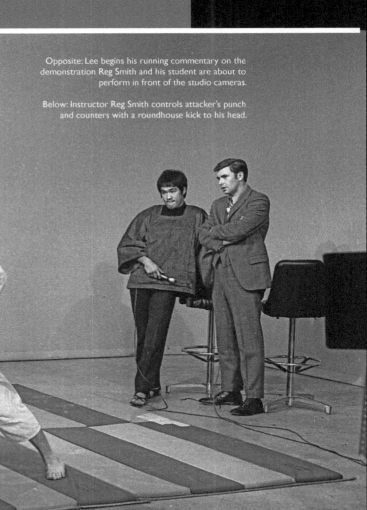

Opposite: Lee begins his running commentary on the demonstration Reg Smith and his student are about to perform in front of the studio cameras.

Below: Instructor Reg Smith controls attacker's punch and counters with a roundhouse kick to his head.

Above: Attacker makes grabbing attack.

Below: Reg Smith demonstrates the application of a double "U-Punch."

Above: Attacker is taken down with arm twist & open-hand strike applied by Smith

Above: After throwing attacker, Smith prepares to make "coup de grace" kick as Lee continues to explain to the show host and television audience the technicalities of the self-defence sequence.

Above: Attacker has been thrown and Smith applies
controlling arm and wrist locks.

Below: Smith moves in past attacker's kick & is
beginning a foot-sweep throw.

Below: SSmith makes a throw following a foot & hand attack. Attacker makes a kicking counter-attack from floor.

Below: Attacker has just been hit by a "Stop-Hit" technique before he could complete his offense and is reeling backwards.

This particular technique is very much the concept behind Lee's own 'Jeet Kune Do' that translates as 'Way of the Intercepting Fist,' as Lee proudly explains to the studio host.

 My biggest regret is that I was unable to take Bruce up on an offer he later made me.

He called and invited me to be in a film they were making in Rome, "The Way of the Dragon."

This movie had the famous fight scene between Bruce and Chuck Norris in the Roman Coliseum.

Bottom: Chuck Norris and Reg Smith at a tournament, 1972.

Bruce said he would create a
fighting scene in which I use
multiple kicks and a high flying kick.
The only problem was, I would have
to pay my own way over.

I had no money back then, and my
wife at the time was totally against me
being in a movie as we had two small
daughters, Paula and Barbie. A missed
opportunity that I can only speculate
on now.

"" After the demo we were approached in the lobby by a local kung fu instructor, Alfredo Sui and his students. He walked up to Bruce and demanded to know why he wasn't selected for the demo since he had a high degree black belt in kung fu. Bruce became angry and yelled, "There are no degrees of black belt in kung fu ! You are a fake ! Get out !"

Above: Sify Alfredo Sui

Bruce then moved forward and the instructor quickly turned and went out the door. My student Howard Herman and I, who were standing with Bruce were quite amused by this exchange.

We then left for a press conference at the Red Carpet Inn, where Bruce was staying in Charlotte.

"

Bruce also taught Lewis how to effectively get in a backfist strike in tournament sparring. In April, 1968, Rhee sponsored the Southeastern Open Karate Championships with promoters Julius Griffith and John Ormsby. This was held at the Park Center in Charlotte, N.C. where Rhee put on a demonstration that stands out the most to me from this

Above: Lee shaking hands with Joe Lewis as Jhoon Rhee stands behind.

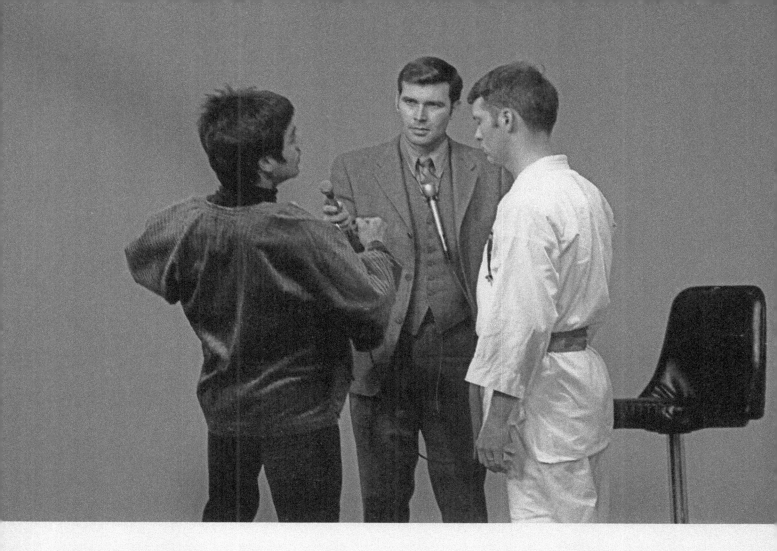

Above: Jhoon Rhee performing his famous kicking agility

event. From a normal standing position he jumped straight up high and threw a front kick straight into his opponent's face and another front kick to his midsection before landing. The audience went wild! One of my students made an 8mm film of this and I studied it over and over as I wanted to do this. I never could and concluded I was too big and heavy to do it. In a later conversation with Rhee, he said he could do it because "his legs were made in Korea."

*" I've always felt
fortunate that I got to
experience his incredible
tactics and the mechanics
of his techniques, even if it
was very brief. How many
people can say they were
beaten up by Bruce Lee ? "
- Reg Smith*

In my professional life I did investigative work and decided to research his background and training. Much later I learned that he used 'Wing Chun' trapping hands to tie me up. In a later phone conversation I asked Bruce about the footwork he used on me. He laughed and said, "Cha Cha."

I had no idea what he meant. It was much later that I learned he had been a Cha Cha dance champion in Hong Kong as a teenager.

Subsequent to that, I worked with a dance instructor to try and figure out his moves. Bruce it seemed had modified the steps and added in a staccato type rhythm to throw off his opponent's timing. Very innovative!

EPILOGUE

DRAGON INN

龍宮飯店

1400 EAST MOREHEAD STREET · CHARLOTTE, N.C.

I took Bruce for a meal at my favorite Chinese restaurant in Charlotte after our television appearance. It was appropriately named "The Dragon Inn." He ordered his favorite, Beef and Scallions in Oyster Sauce. Being the collector I am, I saved the menu he ordered from.

This meal together gave us some time to talk & get to know each other. Bruce was excited about a film he was planning called "The Silent Flute." He said it would be the ultimate film about martial arts philosophy, but he wouldn't give me any details. Bruce initially liked me for my kicking ability.

After we had talked for awhile, he said he liked me because I'd spent much of my life studying Oriental history, culture and philosophy.

This was the beginning of our friendship which continued until his untimely passing in 1973.

- Reg Smith

Below: Bruce Lee, (with Reg Smith to his left) being interviewed by the local press after the television performance. Lee's role in the MGM movie 'Marlowe' was being released in late October in Charlotte.

ACKNOWLEDGEMENTS

The publishers would like to express their sincere thanks to Howard Herman, who as well as being a student of GM Reg Smith, has kindly shared his recollections from being present that day during the WSOC television appearance in October 1969. Although sadly, Howard never appeared in any of the images within this publication, his memories of that day, have greatly enhanced our research into this historical moment in the life of both Reg Smith and Bruce Lee.

LEARN
SELF DEFENSE
AT THE
CENTRAL YMCA

Charlotte Central YMCA Karate Instructor Reg Smith demonstrates technique on TV as film star Bruce Lee narrates.

REG SMITH
2nd DEGREE
BLACK BELT
CHIEF INSTRUCTOR

NOW PLAYING
PARK
TERRACE
THEATRE

Enter The Dragon

BRUCE LEE'S
LAST
and
BEST

Bruce Lee and Reg Smith pause for photographers after press conference on Mr. Lee's forthcoming movies.

MEN AND WOMEN

YOU TOO CAN LEARN QUALITY KARATE FROM CHARLOTTE'S MOST ESTABLISHED SCHOOL OF SELF DEFENSE AT THE CENTRAL YMCA, 400 EAST MOREHEAD STREET.

MONDAYS AND WEDNESDAYS 7:15 TO 9:00 PM

CHIEF INSTRUCTOR REG SMITH, FOREMOST STUDENT OF KOREA'S NATIONAL CHAMPION, MASTER CHUNG KOO KIN, 7th DAN.

MR. SMITH HAS OVER 12 YEARS EXPERIENCE IN ORIENTAL MARTIAL ARTS AND WAS WELL ACQUAINTED WITH THE LATE BRUCE LEE.

THE NAME IN CHARLOTTE KARATE IS . . .
REG SMITH

Flying kick practice by YMCA Assistant Instructor, Andy Jessup, of the Mecklenburg County Police Dept.

"Bruce and I continued to stay in touch, mostly by phone, until his untimely death in 1973. I had made an agreement with him that the school would put on demonstrations at the theaters where his films were playing on opening nights. Our biggest event was for "Enter the Dragon" at the Park Terrace theater. This was a lot of fun and great publicity."
- Reg Smith

CPSIA information can be obtained
at www.ICGtesting.com
Printed in the USA
LVHW071332071021
699809LV00003B/49